By Sabrina Mesko

HEALING MUDRAS
Yoga for Your Hands
Random House - Original edition

POWER MUDRAS
Yoga Hand Postures for Women
Random House - Original edition

MUDRA - Gestures of POWER
DVD - Sounds True

CHAKRA MUDRAS DVD set
HAND YOGA for Vitality, Creativity and Success
HAND YOGA for Concentration, Love and Longevity

HEALING MUDRAS
Yoga for Your Hands - New Edition

HEALING MUDRAS - New Edition in full color:
Healing Mudras I. ~ For Your Body
Healing Mudras II. ~ For Your Mind
Healing Mudras III. ~ For Your Soul

POWER MUDRAS
Yoga Hand Postures for Women - New Edition

MUDRA THERAPY
Hand Yoga for Pain Management and Conquering Illness

YOGA MIND
45 Meditations for Inner Peace, Prosperity and Protection

MUDRAS FOR ASTROLOGICAL SIGNS
Volumes I. ~ XII.
MUDRAS for ARIES, TAURUS, GEMINI, CANCER, LEO, VIRGO,
LIBRA, SCORPIO, SAGITTARIUS, CAPRICORN, AQUARIUS, PISCES
12 Book Series

LOVE MUDRAS
Hand Yoga for Two

MUDRAS AND CRYSTALS
The Alchemy of Energy Protection

THE HOLISTIC CAREGIVER
A Guidebook for at-home care in late stage of Alzheimer's and dementia

MUDRAS
for
CAPRICORN

By Sabrina Mesko Ph.D.H.

The material contained in this book has been written for informational purposes and is not intended as a substitute for medical advice nor is it intended to diagnose, treat, cure, or prevent disease. If you have a medical issue or illness, consult a qualified physician.

A Mudra Hands™ Book
Published by Mudra Hands Publishing

Copyright © 2013 Sabrina Mesko Ph.D.H.

Photography by Mara
Animal photography by Sabrina Mesko
Illustrations by Kiar Mesko
Cover photo by Mara

Printed in the United States of America

ISBN-13:978-0615920955
ISBN-10: 0615920950

For all my Capricorn Friends

TABLE OF CONTENTS

THE MUDRA PRACTICE IS A
COMPLIMENTARY HEALING TECHNIQUE,
THAT OFFERS FAST AND EFFECTIVE
POSITIVE RESULTS.

MUDRAS WORK HARMONIOUSLY
WITH OTHER TRADITIONAL,
ALTERNATIVE AND COMPLEMENTARY
HEALING PROTOCOLS.

THEY HELP RESTORE DEPLETED
SUBTLE ENERGY STATES
AND OPTIMIZE THE PRACTITIONER'S
OVERALL STATE OF WELLNESS.

Mudras for CAPRICORN

DECEMBER 22 - JANUARY 20

BODY
Knees, skin, bones, teeth

PLANET
Saturn

COLORS
Dark gray, black, dark brown

ELEMENT
Earth

STONES and GEMS
Turquoise, amethyst

ANIMAL
Goats

INTRODUCTION

Ever since I can remember, I have been fascinated by the never ending view of the stars in the sky and the presence of other mysterious planets. As a child I wondered for hours about where does the Universe end and when my Father explained the possibility that time and space exist in a very different way than we imagined, my mind went wild with possibilities. I was however quite skeptical about astrology in general until one day in my early youth, a dear friend introduced me to a true Master of Vedic Astrology. He quickly and completely diminished any of my doubts about how precise certain facts can be revealed in one's Celestial map.

It was as if an invisible veil had been removed, and I was granted a peek over to the other side. The astrologer also adamantly pointed out that nothing is written in stone and one's destiny has a lot of space to navigate thru. You can make the best of the situation if you know your given parameters. My fascination and use of astrological science continues to this day and compliments and enriches my work with other observation techniques that I use when consulting.

One is born with character aspects and potential for realization of mapped-out future events, but there is always a possibility that another road may be taken. This has to do with the choices we make. Free will is given to all of us, even though often the choices we have seem to be very limited. But still, the choices are always there, forcing us to consciously participate and eventually take responsibility for our decisions, actions, and consequences.

The science of Astrology has been around for millenniums and even though some people are still doubtful, I always remind them that there is no disputing the fact, that the Moon affects the high and low tide of our Oceans - hence our bodies consisting mostly of water are affected by planetary movements in many fascinating and profound ways. Even the biggest skeptic agrees with that fact.

The Love of the Universal Power for each one of us is unconditional, everlasting and omnipresent. No matter what kind of life-journey you have, it is the very best one designed especially for you, rest assured. And when you are experiencing life's various challenges and wishing for a smooth ride instead, keep in mind that a life filled with lessons is a life fulfilling its purpose. The tests you encounter in your daily life are your opportunities.The wisdom learned is your asset, and the experiences gained are your wealth. Your Spirit's abundance is measured by the battles you fought and how you fought them. Did you help others and leave this world a better place in any way? Your true intention matters more than you know.

Each one of us has a very unique-one of a kind celestial map placed gently, but firmly and irrevocably into effect at the precise time of our birth. There are certain aspects of one's chart that reveal possible character tendencies and predisposed behavior in regards to love, partnerships, maintaining one's health, pursuit of success and a way of communicating. The benefits of knowing and understanding the effects of your chart on various aspects of your life can be profound. It can help you understand and prepare ahead of time for certain circumstances that are coming your way, which increases the possibility of a better quality of life in general.

If you knew that a specific time period could be beneficial for your career wouldn't it be good to know that ahead of your plans? If you are aware that certain aspects of your physical constitution are predisposed to a weakness or sensitivity, wouldn't it be beneficial to pay attention and prevent a possible future health ailment?

If you can foresee that a certain time will be slower for you in achieving positive results, wouldn't it be wise to use that time for preparation for a more fortuitous timing? How many times have you attempted to pursue a dream of yours that just didn't seem to want to happen? And when you were completely exhausted and disillusioned, the fortunate opportunity presented itself, except now you were tired, overwhelmed and had no energy or enthusiasm left. Having such information ahead of time would offer you the chance to save your energy during quiet, less active time, so that when your luck is more likely, you can seize the opportunity and make the most of it. Since writing my first books on Mudras a while ago, my work has expanded into many different areas, however I always included Mudras into my new ventures. When I designed International Wellness and Spa centers, I included Mudra programs to share these beneficial techniques with a wide audience. I included Mudras into my weekly TV show and guided large audiences thru practice on live shows.

Mudras will forever fascinate me and I have been humbled and excited how many practitioners from around the world have written me, grateful to have these techniques and most importantly really experiencing positive effects in time of need. Therefore it has been a natural idea for me to combine these two of my favorite topics and create a series of Mudra sets for all twelve Astrological signs.

The Mudras depicted in this book are specifically selected for the astrological sign of Aries with intention to help you maximize your gifts and soften the challenges that your celestial map contains.

It is important to know that each astrological chart - celestial map-contains information that can be used beneficially and there are no "bad signs" or "better sings". Your chart is unique as are you. By gaining information, knowledge and understanding what the placements of the planets offer you, your path to self knowledge is strengthened.

I hope this book will attract astrology readers as well as meditation and yoga practitioners and help you utilize the beneficial combination of both these fascinating techniques. Knowledge will help you experience the very best possible version of your life. The biggest mystery in your life is You. Discover who you are and enjoy the journey.

And remember, no matter what life presents you with, don't forget to smile and keep a happy heart. With each experience gained you are spiritually wealthier for it. And that my friend, stays with you forever.

The wisdom gained is eternally imprinted in your soul.

Blessings,

Sabrina

MUDRAS

Mudras are movements involving only fingers, hands and arms. Mudras originated in ancient Egypt where they were practiced by high priests and priestesses in sacred rituals. Mudras can be found in every culture of the world. We all use Mudras in our everyday life when gesturing while communicating and when holding our hands in various intuitive positions. Mudras used in yoga practice offer great benefits and have a tremendously positive overall effect on our overall state of well-being. By connecting specific fingertips and your palms in various Mudra positions, you are directly affecting complex energy currents of your subtle energy body. As numerous energy currents run thru your brain centers, Mudras help stimulate specific areas for an overall state of emotional, physical and mental well being.

Instructions for Mudra Practice

YOUR BODY POSTURE
During the Mudra practice sit in an upright position with a straight spine, with both your feet on the ground or in a cross legged position. Comfort is essential so that you may practice undisturbed and focus on proper practice positions.

YOUR EYES
Keep your eyes closed and gently lightly lift the gaze above the horizon.

WHERE
For achieving best results of ideal Mudra practice it is essential that you find a peaceful place, without distractions. Once your Mudra practice is established, you can practice Mudras anywhere.

WHEN

You may practice Mudras at any time. Best times for practice are first thing in the morning and at bedtime. Avoid practicing Mudras on a full stomach, and after a big meal wait for an hour before practice.

HOW LONG

Each Mudra should be practiced for at least 3 minutes at a time. Ideal practice is 3 Mudras for 3 minutes each with a follow up short 3 minutes of complete stillness, peace and meditation or reflection.

HOW OFTEN

You may practice Mudras every day. Explore various Mudras by selecting a Mudra that fits your specific needs for any given day.

BREATH CONTROL

Proper breathing is essential for optimal Mudra practice. There are two main breathing techniques that can be used with your practice.

LONG DEEP SLOW BREATH

Slowly and deeply inhale thru your nose while relaxing and expanding the area or your solar plexus and lower stomach. Exhale thru the nose slowly while gently contracting the stomach area and pulling your stomach in. Pace your breathing slowly and notice the immediate calming effects. This breathing technique is appropriate for relaxation, inducing calmness and peace.

BREATH OF FIRE

Inhale and exhale thru the nose at a much faster pace while practicing the same concept of expanding navel area and contracting with each exhalation. Unless otherwise noted Mudras are generally practiced with the long slow breath. The breath of fire has an energizing, recharging effect on body and is to be used only when so noted.

CHAKRAS

Along our spine, starting at the base and continuing up towards the top of your head, lie subtle energy centers-vortexes-called charkas, that have a powerful effect on the overall state of your health and well being.
The practice of Mudras profoundly affects the proper function of these energy centers and magnifies their power.

Our subtle energy body is highly sensitive to outside sensory stimuli of sound, aromas, visuals and outside electric currents that constantly surround us. Frequencies that permeate specific locations may attract or bother you. Perhaps you may feel eager to stay somewhere where the energy suits you and yet feel suffocated when the environment does not agree with you. We are all sensitive to energies, but some of us feel them more than others.

A positive blend of energies with another person can create a magnet-like effect, whereas another person's negative unharmonious subtle energy field subconsciously pushes you away.

By leading healthy lives and optimizing the proper function of charkas, you empower your subtle energy bodies adding strength to your physical body, mind and spirit. Destructive behavior like addictions and abuse weakens your Auric field and "leaks" your vital energy. By maintaining a healthy Aura-energy field, you can fine-tune your natural capacity for "sensing" places, situations and people that compliment your energy frequency.
In a state of "clean energy" you achieve capacity for high awareness and become your own best guide.

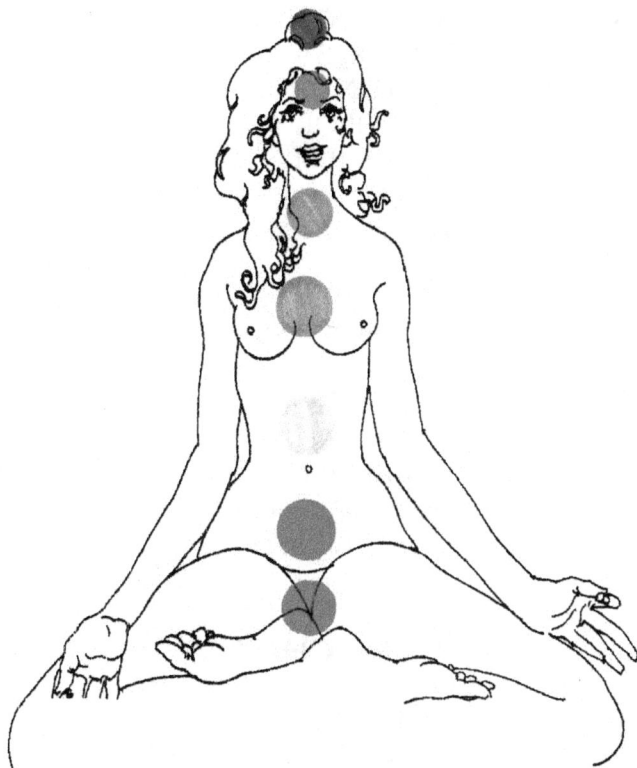

CHAKRAS IN THE BODY

Base Chakra: Foundation
Second Chakra: Sexuality
Third Chakra: Ego
Fourth Chakra: Love
Fifth Chakra: Truth
Sixth Chakra: Intuition
Seventh Chakra: Divine Wisdom

FIRST CHAKRA
LOCATION: Base of the spine
GLAND: Gonad
COLOR: Red
REPRESENTS:
Foundation, shelter, survival,
courage, inner security, vitality

SECOND CHAKRA
LOCATION: Sex organs
GLAND: Adrenal
COLOR: Orange
REPRESENTS:
Creative expression, sexuality,
procreation, family

THIRD CHAKRA
LOCATION: Solar plexus
GLAND: Pancreas
COLOR: Yellow
REPRESENTS:
Ego, intellect, emotions of fear and anger

FOURTH CHAKRA
LOCATION: Heart
GLAND: Thymus
COLOR: Green
REPRESENTS:
All matters of the heart, love,
self–love, compassion and faith

FIFTH CHAKRA
LOCATION: Throat
GLAND: Thyroid
COLOR: Blue
REPRESENTS:
Communication, truth,
higher knowledge, your voice

SIXTH CHAKRA
LOCATION: Third Eye
GLAND: Pineal
COLOR: Indigo
REPRESENTS:
Intuition, inner vision, the Third eye

SEVENTH CHAKRA
LOCATION: Top of the head - Crown
GLAND: Pituitary
COLOR: White and Violet
REPRESENTS:
The universal God consciousness,
the heavens, unity

NADIS

Your subtle energy body contains an amazing network of electric currents called Nadis. There are 72.000 energy currents that run throughout your body from toes to the top of your head as well as your fingertips. These channels of light must be clear and vibrant with life force for your optimal health and empowerment. With regular Mudra practice you can open, clear, reactivate and re-energize your energy currents.

YOUR HANDS AND FINGERS

While practicing Mudras you are magnifying the effects of the Solar system on your physical, mental and spiritual body. Each finger is influenced by the following planets:

THE THUMB - MARS

THE INDEX FINGER - JUPITER

THE MIDDLE FINGER - SATURN

THE RING FINGER – THE SUN

THE LITTLE FINGER - MERCURY

MANTRA

Combining the Mudra practice with appropriate Mantras magnifies the beneficial effects of these ancient self-healing techniques.

The hard palate in your mouth has 58 energy meridian points that connect to and affect your entire body.

By singing, speaking or whispering Mantras, you touch these energy points in a specific order that is beneficial and has a harmonious and healing effect on your physical, mental and spiritual state.

The ancient science of Mantras helps you reactivate nadis, magnifies and empowers your energy field, improves your concentration and stills your mind.

About Astrology

The word Horoscope originates from a Latin word ORA–hour and SCOPOS–view. One could presume that Horoscope means "a look into your hour of birth". The precise moment of your birth determines your celestial set-up.

An accurate astrological chart can reveal most detailed aspects of your life, your character, your gifts, your future possible events, challenges that await you, lucky events that are bestowed upon you, and your outlook for happy relationships, successful careers, accomplishments, health and many possible variations of life events. I say possible, because your decisions will determine the outcome.

There are 12 signs in the Zodiac and your birth-day reflects the position of your Sun sign. The specific positions of other planets in your chart are calculated considering the precise moment-hour and minute and of course location of your birth. The birth time will reveal your Rising or Ascending sign, which will further determine other essential facts of your chart.

The constant transitional movements of the Planets affect each one of us differently, a time that may be difficult for some may prove supremely lucky for another and yet we are interconnected by mutual effects of continuous planetary movements. Nothing is standing still, the changes are ongoing. On a different note, a few slow moving planets connect us in other ways, as they keep certain generations under specific aspects and influences. We are all inseparable and in continuous motion.

There are numerous fascinating ways to use astrology and there is no doubt that the constant motion of all these powerful and majestic Planets in our Solar system affect each and every one of us differently. Astrology can be used as an additional tool to help you continue progressing on the mysterious life journey of self discovery and self-realization.

Remember, the power of decision is yours as is the responsibility for consequences. Make peace with your doubts, pursue your dreams and relish in results.

When the outcome is less than what you expected, learn to pick yourself up and continue on, wiser with knowledge you gained, that alone being a good reason for remaining optimistic. When the outcome surpasses your expectations, well, then you will know what to do…mostly take a breath, smile, and enjoy the moment.

YOUR SUN SIGN

There are 12 signs in the Zodiac. The day of your birth determines your Sun-sign. Most often this is the extent of average person's knowledge and interest in astrology. However, the other aspects in the astrological chart are equally as important and need to be taken into consideration. In this book your main guide is your Sun sign's dispositions, tendencies, weaknesses and gifts. Certainly there are endless combinations of charts and your Sun sign alone will not reveal the complete picture of your celestial map.

For more detailed information and reflection about your chart, you need to know your ascending-rising sign.

Your Ascending-Rising Sign

Your rising sign, also known as the ascendant, reflects the degree of ecliptic rising over the eastern horizon at the precise moment of your birth. It reveals the foundation of your personality. That means that even if you have the same birthday with someone else, your time of birth would create completely different aspects and influences in your chart. No two people are alike. You are one of a kind and so is everyone else. However, you may have some strong similarities and timing aspects that will be often alike. Your rising sign also reveals the basis of your chart and House placements. Your rising sign determines and is in your first house. There are 12 Houses and each depicts precise in-depth information about all aspects of your physical life, emotional make and character tendencies. It is incredibly complex and fascinating. Regarding your Mudra practice in combination with your Astrological Sign, it would be beneficial to know also your Rising sign and apply Mudras that empower your Rising sign as well. For example; if your Sun sign is Aries, but your rising sign is Libra-it would be most beneficial to practice Mudra sets for both signs.

How to use this book

In each book of the *Mudras for the Astrological Signs* series, you will find Mudras for different astrological signs that will help you in most important areas of your life: Health, Love, Success, and Overcoming your challenging qualities. We all have them, as we also all have gifts. This book is specific for the sign of Aries. You may change your Mudra practice daily as needed, and keep in mind, that certain habits or tendencies need a longer time to adjust, change, and improve. Be patient, kind, and loving towards yourself.

MUDRAS FOR TRANSCENDING CHALLENGES

Each one of us has a few character tendencies or weaknesses that are connected to our astrological chart. To help you transcend, overcome and redirect these challenges into your beneficial assets, you can use the Mudras in this chapter.

MUDRAS FOR HEALTH AND BEAUTY

Each astrological sign rules certain areas of your body. The Mudras in this chapter will help you strengthen your physical weaknesses while maintaining a healthy body, and a beautiful, vibrant appearance.

MUDRAS FOR LOVE

The Mudras in this chapter will help you understand your love temperament, your expectations, your longings and how to attract the optimal love partner into your life. It is most beneficial to know how others perceive you in the matters of the heart. It will also help you understand your partner and their astrologically influenced love map.

MUDRAS FOR SUCCESS

The Mudras in this chapter will offer you tools to present yourself to the world in your optimal light. Often one is confused in which direction to turn or where their strength lies. Mudras will help you focus and remember your essential creative desires, help you gain self-confidence and inner security to recognize your desired and destined path. If you know what you want, and your purpose is harmonious for the better good of all, your success is within reach.

MUDRAS
for TRANSCENDING
CHALLENGES

MUDRA FOR OPENING
YOUR CROWN

Your highly driven and hard working nature makes it challenging for you to sit still and go within. You will always get to the top of the mountain, but do remember that it is Divine Will that helped you get there as well as your hard work. Consciously connect and open your crown chakra and let the Universal Divine power nurture, rejuvenate and energize your being. It will be a relief to not always have to do everything yourself and on your own.   If you wish, keep your work associates at a distance, but get closer to the Universe-this connection will be always reliably helpful, and unconditionally loving.

CHAKRA : 7

COLOR: VIOLET

MANTRA:
OM
(God in His Absolute State)

Sit with a straight spine. Lift your hands above your head, all fingers kept apart as if you were holding a crown on your head. Keep the arms at this level and fingers stretched the entire practice. Visualize a stream of bright white light pouring into the crown of your head and filling your entire body with healing light.

BREATH: Long, deep and slow.

MUDRA FOR
RELEASING NEGATIVITY

When things don't instantly go your way, you might have a tendency to let the good feelings turn into pessimistic and cynical thought patterns. Maybe you are feeling responsible somewhere deep down for anything less than perfection. Be still and have a talk with yourself. Who's words are you listening to? Are they yours or maybe from your distant past? Release old pattern's and become free of anything that may be in the way of your vivacious and fun nature. Let your unusual sense of humor entertain you and make light of situation. Everything passes and it will do you good not to take yourself so seriously all the time. This Mudra will help you overcome this tendency and move into a brighter, more optimistic space.

CHAKRA: 4

COLOR: Green

Sit with a straight back. Bend your arms and make fists with both hands. Bring them up in front of your heart. Cross the hands over each other, palms turned outwards. Hold the Mudra across the chest with the left arm on the outer side.

BREATH: Long, deep and slow.

MUDRA
FOR PROTECTION

You lead your close and extended family in addition to your business empire in every and each way and tend to forget to slow down a bit and pay attention to your inner deepest self. You are not alone in this world and even though sometimes your inner child feels forgotten amidst large crowds, remember that you are always protected and loved. Surround yourself with white healing light and practice this Mudra. Make it a part of your regular daily regimen, especially before demanding meetings or projects.

CHAKRA: All

COLOR: All

MANTRA:
OM
(God Is His Absolute State)

Sit with a straight spine. Cross your left hand over your right one and place them on your upper chest. Palms are facing you and all fingers are together. Hold for three minutes and feel the immediate energy shift.

BREATH: Long, deep and slow.

MUDRAS
for HEALTH
and BEAUTY

MUDRA FOR
PROTECTING YOUR HEALTH

Being the hard worker and high achiever that you are, you need to pay just as much attention to keeping your body mind and soul fit, nurtured, healthy and fulfilled. This can not wait till tomorrow when you are fighting off the flu, tending to your family, launching a new project and helping a friend in need. The time is now and every day. First tend to yourself then you can take care of everyone else. Your executive carer positions usually require you to be in your office, so make extra effort to go out into nature where you can truly recharge your body, mind and spirit. It may not seem too practical at the time, but yes, it is worth it.

CHAKRA : All color
COLOR: All color
MANTRA:
OM
(God in His Absolute State)

Sit with a straight back. Bend your right elbow and lift your left hand up, palm facing out. The index and middle fingers are pointing up; the rest are curled with the thumb over them. Hold your left hand in the same Mudra with the two stretched fingers touching your heart. Hold for three minutes.

BREATH: Inhale for ten counts, hold the breath for ten counts, and exhale for ten counts. Pace yourself comfortably, relax and be still.

MUDRA FOR
ANTI AGING

We all know how some people tend to burn themselves out by working so hard it's like they are burning a candle at both ends. Well, you might be one of those people. Your ambition is a great asset and your disciplined nature will help you see any project thru, but you must not forget the essential element-yourself. What is an empire without a leader? So look at this as part of the practical must-do agenda. In order to preserve your youthful glow and recharge your battery, practice this Mudra and keep replenishing your being with everlasting power and indestructible stamina.

CHAKRA : 1, 2

COLOR: Red, orange
MANTRA:

EK ONG KAR SA TA NA MA
(One Creator of Infinity, Birth, Death, and Rebirth)

Sit with a straight back and make circles with your thumbs and index fingers. Stretch out the other fingers and place your hands on your knees, or in front of you-palms facing up.

BREATH: Short, fast breath of fire, focusing on the navel.

MUDRA FOR
STRONG NERVES

Even though you seem to be made of steel, your nerves are delicate and your skin sensitive. Keeping your nerves strong is essential for your health. Do not let all the responsibility and ambition deplete your reservoir of power. Your especially vulnerable areas of knees, bones and teeth need to be guarded as well. Over-extending your workload could cause injury or over loaded nervous system. This Mudra will help you preserve, protect and maintain healthy nerves.

CHAKRA : 3, 4

COLOR: Yellow, Green

Sit with a straight spine and lift your left hand to ear level with palm facing out. Connect the thumb and the middle finger while keeping the other fingers straight. The right hand is in your lap with thumb and little finger touching palm facing up towards the sky. The rest of the fingers are stretched. **The position is REVERSED for men.**

BREATH: Inhale long, deep and slow thru your nose in four counts, and exhale in one strong breath.

MUDRAS
for LOVE

MUDRA FOR LOVE

You like to be in control and falling in love is not one of those things. Suddenly you fell powerless and not the decision maker. Try to not interfere with your heart's journey, and take just as much time for developing the capacity to let it all happen naturally. You can not be in charge all the time. Relax and let love. Consciously get to a place of deep relaxation where you can soften up your invisible barriers and allow the transformative experience of falling in love happen. It may take an additional aspect like intellectual attraction, but love has to have a chance to breathe, grow and transform you. That is all part of the human experience. Allow this Mudra to show you the way.

CHAKRA : 4

COLOR: Green

MANTRA:
SAT NAM WAHE GURU
(God is Truth, His Is the
Supreme Power and Wisdom)

Sit with a straight spine and raise your hands to the either side of your head. Curl the middle and ring fingers into your palm an extend the thumbs, index fingers, and little fingers. Keep your elbows from sinking and hold for three minutes.

BREATH: Inhale for eight short counts, with one strong, long exhale.

MUDRA FOR RELEASING GUILT

There is a slightly controlling streak in your nature. When things do not go according to your envisioned plan, you try to change them to fit your picture. But manipulating anything in the matters of the heart has a high price. Look at love as a beautiful budding flower. You can not decide when it will bloom. Give it some air, sunshine, food, and love and and enjoy the journey. Release the need for feeling responsible for everything and any feelings of guilt that arise when all does not go according to your fantastic plan. There is a better one already written. This Mudra will help you release any feelings of guilt and find that inner calmness you long for. Make space for pure, unconditional, and carefree love.

CHAKRA : 3

COLOR: Yellow

MANTRA:

I AM THINE WAHE GURU
(I am Thine, Divine Teacher within)

Sit with a straight back, elbows out to the sides, and bring your palms up to the level between your stomach and heart center. Palms are facing up toward the sky, right hand resting in left. Upper arms are slightly away from the body. Breathe slowly and deeply.

BREATH: Long, deep and slow.

MUDRA FOR
INNER SECURITY

When you feel insecure in matters of the heart, it is certain that both partners in relationship will pay the price. But remember, no one expects perfection and you are loved just the way you are. The other fact is that while you are quite independent yourself, you need a strong and secure partner at your side. When you want a confident partner, you need to first become one yourself. As you will learn, your carer success has little to do with confidence in matters of the heart. These are two different worlds. Let go of your reserved disposition and prudent inclinations. Just breathe and be free of everything you think you should be. For your lover, all you need to do is just show up. The rest will happen on its own.

CHAKRA: 3, 4

COLOR: Yellow, green

MANTRA:

AD SHAKTI AD SHAKTI
(I Bow to the Creator's Power)

Sit with a straight back, place your hands in reversed prayer pose: hands touching back to back at the level of your heart and solar plexus. Hold the pose for one and a half minutes, then repeat with the palms pressed together in a prayer pose.

BREATH: Long, deep and slow.

MUDRAS
for SUCCESS

MUDRA FOR RELAXATION AND JOY

All that hard work and running families as well as companies will mean nothing if you forget to enjoy it as well. Take a deep breath, stop for a moment and enjoy all that you've created. Being practical does not mean that relaxation is off limits. As a matter of fact, without experiencing some joy for all your efforts and hard work, your life will become very monotone and you will wonder why you feel so dissatisfied. And when you finally go on that long overdue vacation, do not book it solid with activities. Book it solid with nothing but air and laughter. Yes, you can be proud of yourself. Smile.

CHAKRA : 3, 4

COLOR: Yellow, green

MANTRA:

HAREE HAR HAREE HAR
(God in His Creative Aspect)

Sit with a straight back, lift up your hands up in front of your chest. Make a fist with your left hand, tucking the thumb inside. Wrap the right hand around the left and place your right thumb over the base of the left thumb. Concentrate on your third Eye area and hold for three minutes. Later, extend your practice to eleven minutes.

BREATH: Long, deep and slow.

MUDRA FOR HIGHER CONSCIOUSNESS

While you are leading your tribe upward and onward, stop to take a break and know that you will become even a better leader-if that is at all possible-when you tune into your higher consciousness. Infusing some spirituality into your projects would be most important. On the other hand, do not go into the extreme opposite direction and fall into a lazy haze. Finding that perfect balance is the key. No matter what direction you turn, your success will reach new heights if you expand your consciousness and infuse some true otherworldliness into everything you do. This Mudra will help you connect to the ultimate power - your higher consciousness. With clear higher intention you can guide the world to be a better place.

CHAKRA: 3, 7

COLOR: Blue, violet

MANTRA:
OM
(God in His Absolute State)

Sit with a straight back. Put your palms together and extend your elbows to either side. Lift your hands in front of your heart, fingers pointed away from you. Each thumb is on the fleshy mound below the little finger of the same hand. Put the palms together with the right thumb snugly above the left thumb. The bottoms of the hands touch firmly. Hold the hands a few inches away from the body.

BREATH: Long, deep and slow.

MUDRA FOR CREATIVITY

With all that ambition comes responsibility and the need for creative resolutions and endless ideas. How important it is to keep them coming, you know better than anyone else. Do not let your practical side overwhelm you, instead employ your tremendous capacity for patience and discipline. We all know that creativity is not just a simple button you can push and deliver a masterpiece. You do need to go into another consciousness and tap into the Source. Then your creative talents will deliver and all the pieces of the puzzle will come together. This Mudra will help keep your creativity flowing, growing and inspiring others. Also it will help you juggle your schedule - fitting for ten people-that only you are capable of maintaining.

CHAKRA : 6, 7

COLOR: Indigo, violet

MANTRA:
GA DA
(God)

Sit with a straight spine. Connect the thumbs and index fingers, keeping the rest of the fingers straight. Bend your elbows and lift your hands to your sides with palms facing up at a sixty-degree angle to your body. Concentrate on your Third eye and meditate for at least three minutes.

BREATH: Short, fast breath of fire from the navel.

ABOUT THE AUTHOR

SABRINA MESKO PH.D.H. is an International and Los Angeles Times bestselling author of the timeless classic *Healing Mudras - Yoga for your Hands* translated into fourteen languages. She authored over twenty books on Mudras, Mudra Therapy, Mudras and Astrology, Holistic Caregiving, Spirituality and Meditation techniques.

Sabrina holds a Bachelors Degree in Sensory Approaches to Healing, a Masters in Holistic Science, a Doctorate in Ancient and Modern Approaches to Healing, and a Ph.D.H in Healtheoloyy from the American Institute of Holistic Theology. She is board certified from the American Alternative medical Association and American Holistic Health Association. She has been featured in media outlets such as The Los Angeles Times, CNBC News, Cosmopolitan, the cover of London Times Lifestyle, The Discovery Channel documentary on Hands, W magazine, First for Women, Health, Web-MD, Daily News, Focus, Yoga Journal, Australian Women's weekly, Blend, Daily Breeze, New Age, the Roseanne Show and various international live television programs. Her articles have been published in world-wide publications. She hosted her own weekly TV show educating about health, well-being and complementary medicine. She is an executive member of the World Yoga Council and has led numerous international Yoga Therapy educational programs. She directed and produced her interactive double DVD titled *Chakra Mudras* - a Visionary awards finalist.

Sabrina also created award winning international Spa and Wellness Centers and is a motivational keynote conference speaker addressing large audiences all over the world. She is the founder of Arnica Press, a boutique Book Publishing House. Her mission is to discover, mentor, nurture and publish unique authors with a meaningful message, that may otherwise not have an opportunity to be heard. She is the founder of world's only online Mudra Teacher and Mudra Therapy Education, Certification and Mentorship program, with her certified therapists spreading these ancient teachings in over 27 countries around the world.

www.SabrinaMesko.com